Amazing
Animal Life Cycles

by Alix Wood

WINDMILL BOOKS™

New York

Published in 2013 by Windmill Books,
An Imprint of Rosen Publishing
29 East 21st Street, New York, NY 10010

Editor for Alix Wood Books: Mark Sachner
US Editor: Sara Antill
Designer: Alix Wood
Consultant: Sally Morgan

Photo Credits: Cover, 1, 2, 3, 4, 5, 6, 7, 8 (top), 9, 10, 11, 12, 13, 14, 15 (bottom), 16, 18,
19 (top & middle), 20, 21, 22 © Shutterstock; 8 (bottom) © Adam Smith; 15 (top) © Corbis Images;
17 (top) © Paul Franklin/Getty Images; 17 (bottom) © Lindsey Puttock/FLPA; 19 (bottom) © Adolson13

Library of Congress Cataloging-in-Publication Data

Wood, Alix.
 Amazing animal life cycles / by Alix Wood.
   p. cm. — (Wow! wildlife)
 Includes index.
 ISBN 978-1-4488-8100-0 (library binding) — ISBN 978-1-4488-8167-3 (pbk.) —
ISBN 978-1-4488-8171-0 (6-pack)
 1. Animal life cycles—Juvenile literature. I. Title.
 QL49.W694 2013
 591.56—dc23
                                              2012003415

Manufactured in the United States of America

CPSIA Compliance Information: Batch #B1S12WM: For Further Information contact Windmill Books, New York, New York at 1-866-478-0556

Contents

What Is a Life Cycle?

A life cycle is the series of changes an animal goes through from its beginning to adulthood. The life cycles of most animals seem very simple. They are born, they grow up, and they have babies of their own. But some animals change in really amazing ways!

Some young animals look a lot like their parents, just smaller. This elephant calf stays close to its mother for the first three to four years of its life. The adults in the group help look after and teach the young elephant. The calf drinks milk from its mother and will live to be about 70 years old.

Elephants are mammals, like humans. They have young that look like smaller versions of themselves.

Some young animals look very different than their adult forms. Butterflies and moths go through huge changes in how they look as they grow. A big change like this is called **metamorphosis**. They go into a sleeplike state looking one way and emerge looking completely different.

The hickory horned devil caterpillar (left) is a young form of the regal moth (above). They don't look alike at all!

WOW! Clever Nature

Frogs have a very complicated life cycle. Red-eyed tree frogs lay their eggs on the underside of leaves hanging over water. That's tricky! Why? Because when the eggs **hatch**, the little tadpoles will fall into the water, which is the perfect place for them to grow into frogs.

Mammal Life Cycle

Compared to frogs and butterflies, mammals have a very straightforward life cycle. They are born looking a lot like tiny adults. Most mammals are born with hair on their bodies. They drink milk from their mother's body. Most mammals don't lay eggs.

Many of our pets are mammals. This cat is looking after her kitten.

Kittens are born blind and deaf. They are very small. At one month old, they get their first teeth and can start to eat solid food.

WOW! Strange Mammals

The echidna is a mammal that lays eggs! The mom makes a nest and lays a hard-shelled egg in her pouch. After 10 days, the egg will hatch and the mom digs a burrow for the baby. The baby is called a puggle. Echidnas drink their mother's milk from patches on her skin.

Pocket Babies

Marsupials are animals that have special pockets to keep their babies in while they grow. Kangaroos, opossums, and koalas are marsupials. When the baby is first born, it is about the size of a jellybean. The babies are called **joeys**.

Kangaroo joeys use their mother's pouch for up to a year!

A wombat baby in its mother's pouch

Wombats and koalas have pouches that face backward! The mother has special muscles in the pouch that keep the baby from falling out.

When koala joeys are finally out of the pouch, after about six months, most of them spend another six months riding piggyback on their moms! The opossum mother below has quite a few babies. All of them want to hitch a ride!

Mom and baby koala

WOW! "Playing Possum"

The opossum in this photo isn't dead. But it sure looks as if it is! When they are scared, oppossums pretend to be dead. They foam at the mouth, become stiff, and produce a foul-smelling fluid. This is what we mean by **"playing possum."**

Bird Life Cycle

Birds make nests and lay eggs in them. A bird's egg contains enough food to feed the new life growing inside. The hard shell protects the egg and keeps it from drying out. When the bird has grown enough to live on its own, it hatches out of the egg.

WOW! Amazing Spinning Eggs!

Guillemots lay their eggs on rocky cliffs. The eggs are narrow at one end and wide at the other. This shape means the eggs roll around in a circle rather than straight off the cliff if they get bumped!

 **Hornbill Builders**

The female hornbill lays her eggs in a hole in a tree. She and her **mate** then close the hole with mud so she is trapped inside with the eggs. The male feeds her and the hatched chicks through a tiny hole in the mud!

Not all birds nest up high. Common terns nest on the ground. The parents will sit on the eggs until they hatch.

This tern has just hatched out of his egg. You can see his brother starting to peck his way out, too.

The parents will feed the chicks until they are old enough to take care of themselves.

Amazing Egg Cases

Some sharks, **skates**, and other sea ceatures lay egg cases. These cases are like hard sacks that protect the young as they grow. They can come in amazing shapes. Sometimes you can find them washed up on the beach.

Skate egg cases on the beach

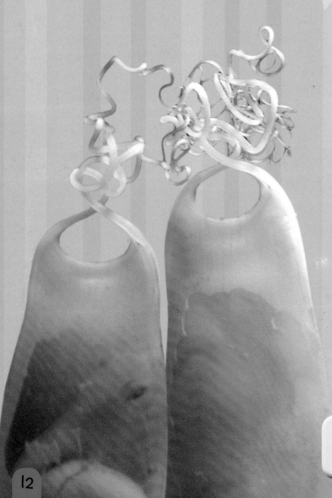

Shark eggs are surrounded by sacks that protect the eggs and the newly hatched pups. The pups take nine months to hatch. The pups look exactly like their parents, only smaller.

In this photo, you can see the sharks growing inside their cases.

This amazing egg case is from a horn shark. The mother wedges the case in gaps in the rock. The screw shape helps it stay there.

WOW! A Mermaid's Necklace?

This amazing string of eggs is from a type of **marine** snail called a whelk. The mother buries one end in the sand, and the rest will float in shallow water. Whelks have a strange life cycle. They begin their lives as males and change to females as they get older!

Parenting in the Oceans

Even though turtles live in the ocean, they lay eggs on land, usually at night. Females may travel long distances to the beach where they were born. A female turtle may lay eggs with hard or soft shells, depending on the type of turtle she is.

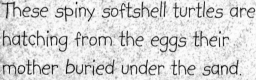

These spiny softshell turtles are hatching from the eggs their mother buried under the sand.

Softshell turtles lay hard-shelled eggs!

Some Like It Hot

If a green turtle's nest is warm, the eggs hatch females. If the nest is cooler, the eggs usually hatch males.

When the hatchlings head to the sea, they don't know where they are going. They follow the light reflected by the water. As they flap along, many **predators**, like gulls and crabs, gather to eat them. Many turtles don't make it.

These newly hatched green turtles are on their dangerous journey to the sea.

Seahorse Dad Plays Mom

The male seahorse has a pouch on his tummy a little like a kangaroo's. The female seahorse puts up to 1,500 eggs in his pouch. He carries the eggs until the baby seahorses hatch.

Frogs and Toads

Frogs have many stages in their life cycle. They change from eggs, to **tadpoles**, to **froglets**, until they become adult frogs. Toads have a very similar life cycle.

Frogs' eggs are called **frog spawn**. Tiny tadpoles come out of the eggs. The tadpoles slowly change. They start to grow back legs, and then front legs. Their tails become smaller. They start to breathe air. Eleven weeks after the eggs were laid, they are fully developed frogs. One day they will mate, and the whole cycle will start again.

Mate

Frog spawn

Frog Life Cycle

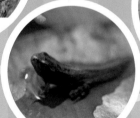
Adult frog

Tadpoles

Froglet

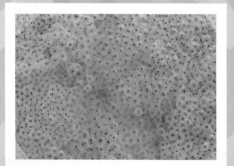

Frogs and toads lay their eggs in special ways to protect them from being eaten. The large, slippery mass of frog spawn is hard for predators to eat. Toads lay their eggs in chains wrapped around plants to keep them safe.

WOW! The Midwife Toad

A male midwife toad with his precious cargo of eggs

The male of some types of midwife toad wraps the string of eggs around his legs and back and carries them around. This keeps them moist and safe from predators. Then, he takes the eggs to water and releases the tadpoles.

Darwin's frogs are good dads. The female lays about 30 eggs. The male guards the eggs for about two weeks, until they hatch. Then, the male takes all the tadpoles into his mouth pouch. The tadpoles develop in his baggy chin skin. When they are ready, they hop out and swim away. Thanks, dad!

A Darwin's frog with a pouch full of babies

Underwater Babies

Dragonflies and damselflies have three stages in their life cycles—the egg, the **nymph**, and the adult. Most of their life is spent in the nymph stage, underwater.

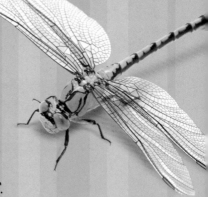

The female dragonfly lays her eggs on a plant in the water. If she can't find a plant, she will just drop them into the water. Nymphs hatch out of the eggs. To our eyes, they look very strange! A dragonfly can stay in the nymph stage for up to four years.

This nymph is changing into a dragonfly. The nymph crawls out of the water and up the stem of a plant. It sheds its skin, and a young dragonfly comes out. It leaves its empty skin stuck to the stem!

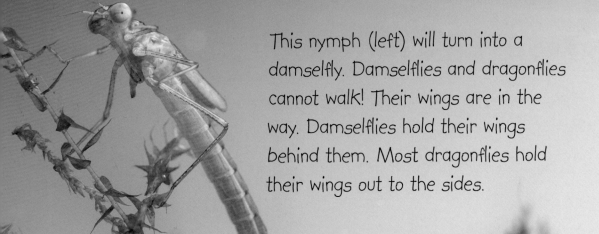

This nymph (left) will turn into a damselfly. Damselflies and dragonflies cannot walk! Their wings are in the way. Damselflies hold their wings behind them. Most dragonflies hold their wings out to the sides.

Damselfly nymph underwater

WOW! Mayfly, Dayfly

Mayflies were once called dayflies, as some only live as an adult for a day or so! In a single day, they have to find a mate. Many mayflies reach adulthood on the exact same day, so they can find a mate. They have been around for about 300 million years. That's long before the dinosaurs existed!

A swarm of mayflies on a car windshield

From an Egg to a Butterfly

In one of the most dramatic changes in nature, a butterfly starts as a tiny, sticky egg. It will then go through several very different stages before it turns into a butterfly. It even wraps itself up in a silk covering!

The female butterfly lays her eggs on plants that the caterpillars, or **larvae,** will later eat. The caterpillars hatch and eat their eggs first. The caterpillars grow fast and shed their skin several times as they grow.

Caterpillars hatching and eating their own eggs

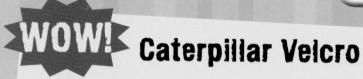 **WOW!** ## Caterpillar Velcro

Caterpillars have six true legs, at the head end. The others are called prolegs. Prolegs have a pad with thousands of tiny hooks that help caterpillars cling to surfaces.

When it has eaten enough, the caterpillar becomes a **pupa**. It finds a branch and spins sticky, silk threads to glue itself to the branch or a leaf. A tough case forms around the caterpillar. This is the pupa. Inside, the caterpillar becomes soft. It starts to turn into a butterfly.

When the pupa becomes see-through, the newly formed butterfly pushes its way out. Its wings are wet and crumpled. It pumps blood into its wings to dry them out.

This monarch butterfly is searching among flowers for food.

Glossary

frog spawn (FRAWG SPAWN)
A mass of fertilized frogs' eggs surrounded by a protective jelly.

froglets (FRAWG-lits)
Young frogs that have recently changed from tadpoles.

hatch (HACH)
To emerge from an egg.

joeys (JOH-eez)
Young marsupials, such as baby kangaroos.

marine (muh-REEN)
From the sea.

marsupials (mahr-SOO-pee-ulz)
Types of mammals that have a pouch on the abdomen of the female where she feeds and carries her young.

mate (MAYT)
One of a breeding pair of animals.

metamorphosis
(meh-tuh-MOR-fuh-sis)
A big change in the form and habits of some animals, as from a tadpole to a frog.

nymph (NIMF)
An immature insect that is smaller than the adult and has undeveloped wings.

playing possum (PLAY-ing PAH-sum)
Pretending to be unconscious or dead when threatened; may also refer to a person pretending to be ignorant.

predators (PREH-duh-terz)
Animals that live by killing and eating other animals.

pupa (PYOO-puh)
The stage or form an insect goes through when changing inside a case from a larva to an adult.

skates (SKAYTS)
Types of fish, related to sharks, with broad, winglike fins.

tadpoles (TAD-pohlz)
The larvae of a frog or toad; a tadpole has a rounded body and a long tail, breathes with gills, and lives in water.

Websites

For web resources related to the subject of this book, go to:
www.windmillbooks.com/weblinks
and select this book's title.

Read More

Fridell, Ron, and Patricia Walsh. *Life Cycle of a Silkworm*. Chicago: Heinemann Library, 2009.

Lawrence, Ellen. *A Kangaroo's Life*. Animal Diaries: Life Cycles. New York: Bearport Publishing, 2012.

Thomson, Ruth. *The Life Cycle of a Frog*. Learning About Life Cycles. New York: PowerKids Press, 2008.

Index